POLESTAR
FAMILY CALENDAR™

Organize · Coordinate · Simplify

ISBN 978-1-55186-120-3

Published by
Polestar Calendars Ltd., 6518 Slocan River Road, Winlaw B.C. Canada V0G 2J0
Phone: 1-800-296-6955 (Canada and U.S.A.) 250-226-7670
www.polestarcalendars.com   Email: info@polestarcalendars.com

Edited by Ruth Porter
Cover illustration by Erin Vanessa – erinvanessa.com
Production and layout by Gillian Stead

This calendar has been printed in Canada on paper made of material
from well-managed FSC®-certified forests, recycled materials,
and other controlled sources

POLESTAR CALENDARS
CREATIVE TIME-MANAGEMENT

www.polestarcalendars.com ★ 1-800-296-6955

User's Guide

POLESTAR FAMILY CALENDAR™ 2022

Welcome!

Welcome to the 2022 edition of *The Polestar Family Calendar*.™ The calendar's format is flexible, so please feel free to customize it to your own purposes. The key is making it work for you and your family.

We'd like to thank all of you for your support, suggestions and encouragement. We believe we have the most committed and enthusiastic customers in the business!

The calendar is available in many retail outlets; you can check our website for a complete listing of Canadian stores that carry our titles. If, however, you can't find it in your local stores we would be happy to fill your order. You'll find the order form in late September; you can phone toll-free at 1-800-296-6955, or order online at www.polestarcalendars.com. We accept Visa or MasterCard.

Daily Calendar Features:

Family Appointments — the place to write down all the meetings, appointments, and special events that your family needs to remember. Encourage older children to write down their own commitments — babysitting schedules, sports practices and games, music lessons, etc.

Meals/Kitchen — design your own best use for this one. Perhaps this will be a menu planner, or the place to record who is doing the daily kitchen chores. You could also use it to note any extra meal guests, or empty places at the table.

Home — tailor this section for your needs, as well. Some people use it for the daily household chores like doing the dishes or taking out the compost, mowing the lawn or shoveling snow. Others use it to note items that need repair, or remind themselves about seasonal home maintenance.

Messages — we've made this section quite large so that phone and other family messages can be marked here each day.

Reference and Record-keeping:

Planning Calendars — two-page calendars for this year and next provide an overview and a place to mark down long-range plans and activities.

Month-at-a-Glance — provides an overview of each month, and is an ideal place to record long-term plans and goals.

Dates to Remember — can be a reminder of annual occasions, a place to record special events or a listing of regularly-scheduled items.

Items Loaned/Borrowed — use these pages to jot down books, tools, and household items you've loaned or borrowed, and record the promised date of return.

Storage Record — can be used to note where you put holiday decorations, seldom-used sports equipment or seasonal equipment, plus the location of important documents such as warranties, insurance policies, wills.

Tear-out Shopping lists — a section of tear-out shopping lists, printed on perforated pages, appears at the very back of the calendar.

Other Polestar Publications:

For a detailed look at our other titles please visit our website at **www.polestarcalendars.com**

Polestar Business Agenda — a complete time-management system for your working life. Includes a week-at-a-glance format, monthly planning and expense pages, plus encouraging weekly quotes. 8"x10", spiral.

Original Student Calendar — runs on the school year, August to August and is ideal for university and high school students. It features an easy-to-use time-management system and includes term timetables, monthly planners and budgeting pages, weekly quotes and illustrations. 6"x 9", spiral.

Polestar Planner — a portable, personal organizer. Week-at-a-glance format with monthly planning pages, address pages, and a large notes section. Also features two inside cover pockets for receipts, etc. 6" x 9", spiral.

We greatly appreciate your letters of support, and your suggestions.
Have a great year!

Ruth Porter and Julian Ross, Publishers

2022 Planning Calendar

JANUARY

S	M	T	W	T	F	S
						1
2	3	4	5	6	7	8
9	10	11	12	13	14	15
16	17	18	19	20	21	22
23	24	25	26	27	28	29
30	31					

FEBRUARY

S	M	T	W	T	F	S
		1	2	3	4	5
6	7	8	9	10	11	12
13	14	15	16	17	18	19
20	**21**	22	23	24	25	26
27	28					

MARCH

S	M	T	W	T	F	S
		1	2	3	4	5
6	7	8	9	10	11	12
13	14	15	16	17	18	19
20	21	22	23	24	25	26
27	28	29	30	31		

APRIL

S	M	T	W	T	F	S
					1	2
3	4	5	6	7	8	9
10	11	12	13	14	**15**	16
17	18	19	20	21	22	23
24	25	26	27	28	29	30

MAY

S	M	T	W	T	F	S
1	2	3	4	5	6	7
8	9	10	11	12	13	14
15	16	17	18	19	20	21
22	**23**	24	25	26	27	28
29	**30**	31				

JUNE

S	M	T	W	T	F	S
			1	2	3	4
5	6	7	8	9	10	11
12	13	14	15	16	17	18
19	20	21	22	23	24	25
26	27	28	29	30		

2022 Planning Calendar

JULY

S	M	T	W	T	F	S
					1	2
3	**4**	5	6	7	8	9
10	11	12	13	14	15	16
17	18	19	20	21	22	23
24	25	26	27	28	29	30
31						

AUGUST

S	M	T	W	T	F	S
	1	2	3	4	5	6
7	8	9	10	11	12	13
14	15	16	17	18	19	20
21	22	23	24	25	26	27
28	29	30	31			

SEPTEMBER

S	M	T	W	T	F	S
				1	2	3
4	**5**	6	7	8	9	10
11	12	13	14	15	16	17
18	19	20	21	22	23	24
25	26	27	28	29	30	

OCTOBER

S	M	T	W	T	F	S
						1
2	3	4	5	6	7	8
9	**10**	11	12	13	14	15
16	17	18	19	20	21	22
23	24	25	26	27	28	29
30	31					

NOVEMBER

S	M	T	W	T	F	S
		1	2	3	4	5
6	7	8	9	10	**11**	12
13	14	15	16	17	18	19
20	21	22	23	**24**	25	26
27	28	29	30			

DECEMBER

S	M	T	W	T	F	S
				1	2	3
4	5	6	7	8	9	10
11	12	13	14	15	16	17
18	19	20	21	22	23	24
25	**26**	27	28	29	30	31

January 2022

SUNDAY	MONDAY	TUESDAY	WEDNESDAY	THURSDAY	FRIDAY	SATURDAY
DECEMBER S M T W T F S 　　　 1 2 3 4 5 6 7 8 9 10 11 12 13 14 15 16 17 18 19 20 21 22 23 24 **25** **26** 27 28 29 30 31	**FEBRUARY** S M T W T F S 　 1 2 3 4 5 6 7 8 9 10 11 12 13 14 15 16 17 18 19 20 **21** 22 23 24 25 26 27 28					*New Year's Day* 1
New Moon ● 2	3	4	5	6	7	8
9	10	11	12	13	14	15
16	*Martin Luther King, Jr. Day (U.S.), Full Moon* ○ 17	18	19	20	21	22
23	24	25	26	27	28	29
30	*New Moon* ● 31					

anuary 2022

O DO THIS MONTH

NEW PROJECTS/IDEAS

NOTES

December/January

Family Appointments	Meals / Kitchen	Home	To Do
27 Monday			
28 Tuesday			
29 Wednesday			
30 Thursday			
31 Friday *New Year's Eve*			

DECEMBER 2021

S	M	T	W	T	F	S
			1	2	3	4
5	6	7	8	9	10	11
12	13	14	15	16	17	18
19	20	21	22	23	24	**25**
26	**27**	**28**	**29**	**30**	**31**	

JANUARY 2022

S	M	T	W	T	F	S
						1
2	3	4	5	6	7	8
9	10	11	12	13	14	15
16	17	18	19	20	21	22
23_{30} 24_{31}	25	26	27	28	29	

And peace begins with a smile.

Mother Teresa,
MONASTIC & HUMANITARIAN
(1910-1997)

Family Appointments	Meals / Kitchen	Home
1 Saturday *New Year's Day*		
2 Sunday ● *New Moon*		

Messages

January

Family Appointments	Meals / Kitchen	Home	To Do
3 Monday			
4 Tuesday			
5 Wednesday			
6 Thursday			
7 Friday			

JANUARY 2022

S	M	T	W	T	F	S
						1
2	**3**	**4**	**5**	**6**	**7**	**8**
9	10	11	12	13	14	15
16	17	18	19	20	21	22
23 30	24 31	25	26	27	28	29

I'm never sure what's coming next, but I'm an open-minded person and I welcome any challenge.

Sarah Polley, DIRECTOR & SCREENWRITER (1979-)

Family Appointments	Meals / Kitchen	Home
8 Saturday		
9 Sunday		

Messages

January

Family Appointments	Meals / Kitchen	Home	To Do
10 Monday			
11 Tuesday			
12 Wednesday			
13 Thursday			
14 Friday			

JANUARY 2022

S	M	T	W	T	F	S
						1
2	3	4	5	6	7	8
9	**10**	**11**	**12**	**13**	**14**	**15**
16	17	18	19	20	21	22
23 30	24 31	25	26	27	28	29

It is more fun to talk with someone who doesn't use long, difficult words but rather short, easy words, like 'What about lunch?'

A.A. Milne, WRITER (1882-1956)

Family Appointments	Meals / Kitchen	Home
15 Saturday		
16 Sunday		

Messages

January

Family Appointments	Meals / Kitchen	Home	To Do
17 Monday *Martin Luther King, Jr. Day (U.S.), ○ Full Moon*			
18 Tuesday			
19 Wednesday			
20 Thursday			
21 Friday			

JANUARY 2022

S	M	T	W	T	F	S
						1
2	3	4	5	6	7	8
9	10	11	12	13	14	15
16	**17**	**18**	**19**	**20**	**21**	**22**
2330	24 31	25	26	27	28	29

Don't ask kids what they want to be when they
grow up; ask them what problem they want to solve.

Jaime Casap, TECHNOLOGY EDUCATOR (1968-)

Family Appointments	Meals / Kitchen	Home
22 Saturday		
23 Sunday		

Messages

January

Family Appointments	Meals / Kitchen	Home	To Do
24 Monday			
25 Tuesday			
26 Wednesday			
27 Thursday			
28 Friday			

JANUARY 2022

S	M	T	W	T	F	S
						1
2	3	4	5	6	7	8
9	10	11	12	13	14	15
16	17	18	19	20	21	22
23/30	24/31	**25**	**26**	**27**	**28**	**29**

Imagine what you would like to see happen,
and then don't do anything to make it impossible.

Ron Padgett, POET (1942-)

Family Appointments	Meals / Kitchen	Home

29 Saturday

30 Sunday

Messages

February 2022

SUNDAY	MONDAY	TUESDAY	WEDNESDAY	THURSDAY	FRIDAY	SATURDAY
		Chinese New Year (Year of the Tiger) **1**	*Groundhog Day* **2**	3	4	5
6	7	8	9	10	11	12
13	*Valentine's Day* **14**	15	*Full Moon* ○ **16**	17	18	19
20	*Family/Heritage Day (Canada), Presidents' Day (U.S.)* **21**	22	23	24	25	26
27	28					

JANUARY

S	M	T	W	T	F	S
						1
2	3	4	5	6	7	8
9	10	11	12	13	14	15
16	17	18	19	20	21	22
23	24	25	26	27	28	29
30	31					

MARCH

S	M	T	W	T	F	S
		1	2	3	4	5
6	7	8	9	10	11	12
13	14	15	16	17	18	19
20	21	22	23	24	25	26
27	28	29	30	31		

February 2022

NEW PROJECTS/IDEAS

NOTES

January/February

Family Appointments	Meals / Kitchen	Home	To Do
31 Monday ● *New Moon*			
1 Tuesday *Chinese New Year (Year of the Tiger)*			
2 Wednesday *Groundhog Day*			
3 Thursday			
4 Friday			

JANUARY 2022

S	M	T	W	T	F	S
						1
2	3	4	5	6	7	8
9	10	11	12	13	14	15
16	17	18	19	20	21	22
23 30	24 31	25	26	27	28	29

FEBRUARY 2022

S	M	T	W	T	F	S
		1	**2**	**3**	**4**	**5**
6	7	8	9	10	11	12
13	14	15	16	17	18	19
20	**21**	22	23	24	25	26
27	28					

A good laugh and a long sleep are the two best cures for everything.

Irish proverb

Family Appointments	Meals / Kitchen	Home
5 Saturday		
6 Sunday		

Messages

February

Family Appointments	Meals / Kitchen	Home	To Do
7 Monday			
8 Tuesday			
9 Wednesday			
10 Thursday			
11 Friday			

FEBRUARY 2022

S	M	T	W	T	F	S
		1	2	3	4	5
6	**7**	**8**	**9**	**10**	**11**	**12**
13	14	15	16	17	18	19
20	**21**	22	23	24	25	26
27	28					

There's really no honour in proving that you can carry the entire load on your own shoulders. And… it's lonely.

Amanda Palmer, ARTIST (1976-)

Family Appointments	Meals / Kitchen	Home
12 Saturday		
13 Sunday		

Messages

February

Family Appointments	Meals / Kitchen	Home	To Do
14 Monday *Valentine's Day*			
15 Tuesday			
16 Wednesday ○ *Full Moon*			
17 Thursday			
18 Friday			

To Buy

FEBRUARY 2022

S	M	T	W	T	F	S
		1	2	3	4	5
6	7	8	9	10	11	12
13	**14**	**15**	**16**	**17**	**18**	**19**
20	**21**	22	23	24	25	26
27	28					

Truly, a little love-making is a very pleasant thing.

L.E. Landon, POET (1802-1838)

Family Appointments	Meals / Kitchen	Home
19 Saturday		
20 Sunday		

Messages

February

Family Appointments	Meals / Kitchen	Home	To Do
21 Monday *Family/Heritage Day (Canada), Presidents' Day (U.S.)*			
22 Tuesday			
23 Wednesday			
24 Thursday			
25 Friday			

FEBRUARY 2022

S	M	T	W	T	F	S
		1	2	3	4	5
6	7	8	9	10	11	12
13	14	15	16	17	18	19
20	**21**	**22**	**23**	**24**	**25**	**26**
27	28					

The fact that you couldn't grow new brain cells, that was a myth. We can do this and it can happen at any age.

Dr. Sanjay Gupta, NEUROSURGEON (1969-)

Family Appointments	Meals / Kitchen	Home
26 Saturday		
27 Sunday		

Messages

March 2022

SUNDAY	MONDAY	TUESDAY	WEDNESDAY	THURSDAY	FRIDAY	SATURDAY
FEBRUARY S M T W T F S 1 2 3 4 5 6 7 8 9 10 11 12 13 14 15 16 17 18 19 20 **21** 22 23 24 25 26 27 28		1	*Ash Wednesday, New Moon* ● 2	3	4	5
6	7	*International Women's Day* 8	9	10	11	12
Daylight Saving Time begins 13	14	15	16	*Purim, St. Patrick's Day* 17	*Full Moon* ○ 18	*Holi* 19
Vernal Equinox 20	21	22	23	24	25	26
27	28	29	30	31	**APRIL** S M T W T F S 1 2 3 4 5 6 7 8 9 10 11 12 13 14 **15** 16 **17** 18 19 20 21 22 23 24 25 26 27 28 29 30	

March 2022

TO DO THIS MONTH

NEW PROJECTS/IDEAS

NOTES

February/March

Family Appointments	Meals / Kitchen	Home	To Do
28 Monday			
1 Tuesday			
2 Wednesday *Ash Wednesday,* ● *New Moon*			
3 Thursday			
4 Friday			

FEBRUARY 2022						
S	M	T	W	T	F	S
		1	2	3	4	5
6	7	8	9	10	11	12
13	14	15	16	17	18	19
20	**21**	22	23	24	25	26
27	**28**					

MARCH 2022						
S	M	T	W	T	F	S
		1	**2**	**3**	**4**	**5**
6	7	8	9	10	11	12
13	14	15	16	17	18	19
20	21	22	23	24	25	26
27	28	29	30	31		

Focus on being productive instead of busy.

Tim Ferriss, ENTREPRENEUR (1977-)

Family Appointments	Meals / Kitchen	Home
5 Saturday		
6 Sunday		

Messages

March

Family Appointments	Meals / Kitchen	Home	To Do
7 Monday			
8 Tuesday *International Women's Day*			
9 Wednesday			
10 Thursday			
11 Friday			

MARCH 2022

S	M	T	W	T	F	S
		1	2	3	4	5
6	**7**	**8**	**9**	**10**	**11**	**12**
13	14	15	16	17	18	19
20	21	22	23	24	25	26
27	28	29	30	31		

I didn't inherit a great wish to be an activist. I was pushed into it by things that were just so outrageous.

Jane Jacobs, JOURNALIST (1916-2006)

Family Appointments	Meals / Kitchen	Home
12 Saturday		
13 Sunday *Daylight Saving Time begins*		

Messages

March

Family Appointments	Meals / Kitchen	Home	To Do
14 Monday			
15 Tuesday			
16 Wednesday			
17 Thursday *Purim, St. Patrick's Day*			
18 Friday ○ *Full Moon*			

MARCH 2022						
S	M	T	W	T	F	S
		1	2	3	4	5
6	7	8	9	10	11	12
13	**14**	**15**	**16**	**17**	**18**	**19**
20	21	22	23	24	25	26
27	28	29	30	31		

Movement is a renewable resource, but it renews through use. Your future movement is made possible by movements you're doing today.

Katy Bowman, BIOMECHANIST (1976-)

Family Appointments	Meals / Kitchen	Home
19 Saturday *Holi*		
20 Sunday *Vernal Equinox*		

Messages

March

Family Appointments	Meals / Kitchen	Home	To Do
21 Monday			
22 Tuesday			
23 Wednesday			
24 Thursday			
25 Friday			

MARCH 2022						
S	M	T	W	T	F	S
		1	2	3	4	5
6	7	8	9	10	11	12
13	14	15	16	17	18	19
20	**21**	**22**	**23**	**24**	**25**	**26**
27	28	29	30	31		

There's no better way to cheer people up than to talk about birds.

Terry Glavin, JOURNALIST (1955-)

Family Appointments	Meals / Kitchen	Home
26 Saturday		
27 Sunday		

Messages

April 2022

SUNDAY	MONDAY	TUESDAY	WEDNESDAY	THURSDAY	FRIDAY	SATURDAY
MARCH S M T W T F S 　 　 1 2 3 4 5 6 7 8 9 10 11 12 13 14 15 16 17 18 19 20 21 22 23 24 25 26 27 28 29 30 31	**MAY** S M T W T F S 1 2 3 4 5 6 7 8 9 10 11 12 13 14 15 16 17 18 19 20 21 22 **23** 24 25 26 27 28 29 **30** 31				*New Moon* ● 1	2
First day of Ramadan 3	4	5	6	7	8	9
Palm Sunday 10	11	12	13	14	*Good Friday* 15	*First day of Passover, Full Moon* ○ 16
Easter 17	18	19	20	21	*Earth Day* 22	23
24	25	26	27	28	29	*New Moon* ● 30

pril 2022

DO THIS MONTH

EW PROJECTS/IDEAS

NOTES

March/April

Family Appointments	Meals / Kitchen	Home
28 Monday		
29 Tuesday		
30 Wednesday		
31 Thursday		
1 Friday ● *New Moon*		

To Do

MARCH 2022						
S	M	T	W	T	F	S
		1	2	3	4	5
6	7	8	9	10	11	12
13	14	15	16	17	18	19
20	21	22	23	24	25	26
27	**28**	**29**	**30**	**31**		

APRIL 2022						
S	M	T	W	T	F	S
					1	**2**
3	4	5	6	7	8	9
10	11	12	13	14	**15**	16
17	18	19	20	21	22	23
24	25	26	27	28	29	30

Be not afraid of going slowly,
be afraid of standing still.

Patrice Nagley,
LIBRARIAN (1921-2015)

Family Appointments	Meals / Kitchen	Home

2 Saturday

3 Sunday   *First day of Ramadan*

Messages

April

Family Appointments	Meals / Kitchen	Home	To Do
4 Monday			
5 Tuesday			
6 Wednesday			
7 Thursday			
8 Friday			

APRIL 2022						
S	M	T	W	T	F	S
					1	2
3	**4**	**5**	**6**	**7**	**8**	**9**
10	11	12	13	14	**15**	16
17	18	19	20	21	22	23
24	25	26	27	28	29	30

Kids keep you very close to experiences. You're kind of constantly thrown off track and that's good….

Deborah Digges, POET (1950-2009)

Family Appointments	Meals / Kitchen	Home
9 Saturday		
10 Sunday *Palm Sunday*		

Messages

April

Family Appointments	Meals / Kitchen	Home	To Do
11 Monday			
12 Tuesday			
13 Wednesday			
14 Thursday			
15 Friday *Good Friday*			

APRIL 2022

S	M	T	W	T	F	S
					1	2
3	4	5	6	7	8	9
10	**11**	**12**	**13**	**14**	**15**	**16**
17	18	19	20	21	22	23
24	25	26	27	28	29	30

Ideas are like rabbits. You get a couple and learn how to handle them, and pretty soon you have a dozen.

John Steinbeck, WRITER (1902-1968)

Family Appointments	Meals / Kitchen	Home

16 Saturday *First day of Passover,* ○ *Full Moon*

17 Sunday *Easter*

Messages

April

Family Appointments	Meals / Kitchen	Home	To Do
18 Monday			
19 Tuesday			
20 Wednesday			
21 Thursday			
22 Friday *Earth Day*			

APRIL 2022

S	M	T	W	T	F	S
					1	2
3	4	5	6	7	8	9
10	11	12	13	14	**15**	16
17	**18**	**19**	**20**	**21**	**22**	**23**
24	25	26	27	28	29	30

And then we'll take up our shovels and get to practical work: digging the pond, planting the world that we want, and singing as we go.

Robin Wall Kimmerer, BOTANIST & WRITER (1953-)

Family Appointments	Meals / Kitchen	Home

23 Saturday

24 Sunday

Messages

May 2022

SUNDAY	MONDAY	TUESDAY	WEDNESDAY	THURSDAY	FRIDAY	SATURDAY
1	2	3	4	5	6	7
Mother's Day (Canada, U.S.) 8	9	10	11	12	13	14
Full Moon ○ 15	16	17	18	19	20	21
22	*Victoria Day (Canada)* 23	24	25	26	27	28
29	*Memorial Day (U.S.), New Moon* ● 30	31				

APRIL

S	M	T	W	T	F	S
					1	2
3	4	5	6	7	8	9
10	11	12	13	14	**15**	16
17	18	19	20	21	22	23
24	25	26	27	28	29	30

JUNE

S	M	T	W	T	F	S
			1	2	3	**4**
5	6	7	8	9	10	11
12	13	14	15	16	17	18
19	20	21	22	23	24	25
26	27	28	29	30		

DO THIS MONTH

W PROJECTS/IDEAS

NOTES

April/May

Family Appointments	Meals / Kitchen	Home	To Do
25 Monday			
26 Tuesday			
27 Wednesday			
28 Thursday			
29 Friday			

APRIL 2022						
S	M	T	W	T	F	S
					1	2
3	4	5	6	7	8	9
10	11	12	13	14	**15**	16
17	18	19	20	21	22	23
24	**25**	**26**	**27**	**28**	**29**	**30**

MAY 2022						
S	M	T	W	T	F	S
1	2	3	4	5	6	7
8	9	10	11	12	13	14
15	16	17	18	19	20	21
22	**23**	24	25	26	27	28
29	**30**	31				

The flowers of late winter and early spring occupy places in our hearts well out of proportion to their size.

Gertrude S. Wister,
HORTICULTURIST (1905-1999)

Family Appointments	Meals / Kitchen	Home
30 Saturday ● *New Moon*		
1 Sunday		

Messages

May

Family Appointments	Meals / Kitchen	Home	To Do
2 Monday			
3 Tuesday			
4 Wednesday			
5 Thursday			
6 Friday			

POLESTAR FAMILY CALENDAR ™

MAY 2022

S	M	T	W	T	F	S
1	**2**	**3**	**4**	**5**	**6**	**7**
8	9	10	11	12	13	14
15	16	17	18	19	20	21
22	**23**	24	25	26	27	28
29	**30**	31				

Only take unpaid work if it's for your mum.

Matt Dowling, CHEF (1945-)

Family Appointments	Meals / Kitchen	Home

7 Saturday

8 Sunday   *Mother's Day (Canada, U.S.)*

Messages

May

Family Appointments	Meals / Kitchen	Home	To Do
9 Monday			
10 Tuesday			
11 Wednesday			
12 Thursday			
13 Friday			

MAY 2022

S	M	T	W	T	F	S
1	2	3	4	5	6	7
8	**9**	**10**	**11**	**12**	**13**	**14**
15	16	17	18	19	20	21
22	**23**	24	25	26	27	28
29	**30**	31				

The most successful people are those who are good at plan B.

James Yorke, MATHEMATICIAN (1941-)

Family Appointments	Meals / Kitchen	Home
14 Saturday		
15 Sunday ○ *Full Moon*		

Messages

May

Family Appointments	Meals / Kitchen	Home	To Do
16 Monday			
17 Tuesday			
18 Wednesday			
19 Thursday			
20 Friday			

To Buy

MAY 2022

S	M	T	W	T	F	S
1	2	3	4	5	6	7
8	9	10	11	12	13	14
15	**16**	**17**	**18**	**19**	**20**	**21**
22	**23**	24	25	26	27	28
29	**30**	31				

It is braver to knock on the door of your next-door neighbour unannounced than to travel half-way round the world.

G.K. Chesterton, WRITER (1874-1936)

Family Appointments	Meals / Kitchen	Home
21 Saturday		
22 Sunday		

Messages

May

Family Appointments	Meals / Kitchen	Home	To Do
23 Monday *Victoria Day (Canada)*			
24 Tuesday			
25 Wednesday			
26 Thursday			
27 Friday			

MAY 2022						
S	M	T	W	T	F	S
1	2	3	4	5	6	7
8	9	10	11	12	13	14
15	16	17	18	19	20	21
22	**23**	**24**	**25**	**26**	**27**	**28**
29	**30**	31				

What I believe is that all clear-minded people should remain two things throughout their lifetimes: curious and teachable.

Roger Ebert, FILM CRITIC & JOURNALIST (1942-2013)

Family Appointments	Meals / Kitchen	Home
28 Saturday		
29 Sunday		

Messages

June 2022

SUNDAY	MONDAY	TUESDAY	WEDNESDAY	THURSDAY	FRIDAY	SATURDAY
MAY S M T W T F S 1 2 3 4 5 6 7 8 9 10 11 12 13 14 15 16 17 18 19 20 21 22 **23** 24 25 26 27 28 29 **30** 31		1	2	3		4
5	6	7	8	9	10	11
12	13	*Full Moon* ○ 14	15	16	17	18
Father's Day (Canada, U.S.) 19	20	*National Indigenous Peoples Day (Canada), Summer Solstice* 21	22	23	*St. Jean Baptiste Day (Canada)* 24	25
26	27	*New Moon* ● 28	29	30	**JULY** S M T W T F S 1 2 3 **4** 5 6 7 8 9 10 11 12 13 14 15 16 17 18 19 20 21 22 23 24 25 26 27 28 29 30 31	

ne 2022

DO THIS MONTH

EW PROJECTS/IDEAS

NOTES

May/June

Family Appointments	Meals / Kitchen	Home	To Do
30 Monday *Memorial Day (U.S.),* ● *New Moon*			
31 Tuesday			
1 Wednesday			
2 Thursday			
3 Friday			

To Buy

MAY 2022

S	M	T	W	T	F	S
1	2	3	4	5	6	7
8	9	10	11	12	13	14
15	16	17	18	19	20	21
22	**23**	24	25	26	27	28
29	**30**	**31**				

JUNE 2022

S	M	T	W	T	F	S
			1	**2**	**3**	**4**
5	6	7	8	9	10	11
12	13	14	15	16	17	18
19	20	21	22	23	24	25
26	27	28	29	30		

Put a stout heart
to a steep hillside.

Sandy Stevenson,
ARTIST & ADVENTURER (1948-2016)

Family Appointments	Meals / Kitchen	Home
4 Saturday		
5 Sunday		

Messages

June

Family Appointments	Meals / Kitchen	Home	To Do
6 Monday			
7 Tuesday			
8 Wednesday			
9 Thursday			
10 Friday			

To Buy

JUNE 2022

S	M	T	W	T	F	S
			1	2	3	4
5	**6**	**7**	**8**	**9**	**10**	**11**
12	13	14	15	16	17	18
19	20	21	22	23	24	25
26	27	28	29	30		

A rainy day is the perfect time for a walk in the woods.

Rachel Carson, BIOLOGIST & CONSERVATIONIST (1907-1964)

Family Appointments	Meals / Kitchen	Home
11 Saturday		
12 Sunday		

Messages

June

Family Appointments	Meals / Kitchen	Home	To Do
13 Monday			
14 Tuesday ○ *Full Moon*			
15 Wednesday			
16 Thursday			
17 Friday			

JUNE 2022

S	M	T	W	T	F	S
			1	2	3	4
5	6	7	8	9	10	11
12	**13**	**14**	**15**	**16**	**17**	**18**
19	20	21	22	23	24	25
26	27	28	29	30		

My father pointed to the moon and asked me what colour it was. I couldn't tell. So he told me to look at the horizon and then glance back quickly at the moon. Then I saw it: it was pale green!

Alden Baker, (20TH C.)

Family Appointments	Meals / Kitchen	Home

18 Saturday

19 Sunday   *Father's Day (Canada, U.S.)*

Messages

June

Family Appointments	Meals / Kitchen	Home	To Do
20 Monday			
21 Tuesday *National Indigenous Peoples Day (Canada), Summer Solstice*			
22 Wednesday			
23 Thursday			
24 Friday *St. Jean Baptiste Day (Canada)*			

JUNE 2022

S	M	T	W	T	F	S
			1	2	3	4
5	6	7	8	9	10	11
12	13	14	15	16	17	18
19	**20**	**21**	**22**	**23**	**24**	**25**
26	27	28	29	30		

When the frogs dream, and the grass waves, and the buttercups toss their heads… then is summer begun.

Henry David Thoreau, NATURALIST & WRITER (1817-1862)

Family Appointments	Meals / Kitchen	Home
25 Saturday		
26 Sunday		

Messages

July 2022

SUNDAY	MONDAY	TUESDAY	WEDNESDAY	THURSDAY	FRIDAY	SATURDAY
					Canada Day 1	2
3	*Independence Day (U.S.)* 4	5	6	7	8	9
10	11	12	*Full Moon* ○ 13	14	15	16
17	18	19	20	21	22	23
24	25	26	27	*New Moon* ● 28	29	30
31						

JUNE

S	M	T	W	T	F	S
			1	2	3	4
5	6	7	8	9	10	11
12	13	14	15	16	17	18
19	20	21	22	23	24	25
26	27	28	29	30		

AUGUST

S	M	T	W	T	F	S
	1	2	3	4	5	6
7	8	9	10	11	12	13
14	15	16	17	18	19	20
21	22	23	24	25	26	27
28	29	30	31			

July 2022

TO DO THIS MONTH

NEW PROJECTS/IDEAS

NOTES

June/July

Family Appointments	Meals / Kitchen	Home	To Do
27 Monday			
28 Tuesday ● *New Moon* Promotion (1 hr) Pictures ~~Paperwork~~ Emails Presents & Food Camming / Set up Computer Nathaniels / Mail NSLSC			
29 Wednesday Grandpas Birthday			
30 Thursday			
1 Friday *Canada Day*			

JUNE 2022

S	M	T	W	T	F	S
			1	2	3	4
5	6	7	8	9	10	11
12	13	14	15	16	17	18
19	20	21	22	23	24	25
26	**27**	**28**	**29**	**30**		

JULY 2022

S	M	T	W	T	F	S
					1	**2**
3	**4**	5	6	7	8	9
10	11	12	13	14	15	16
17	18	19	20	21	22	23
24/31	25	26	27	28	29	30

Twice I have lived forever
in a smile.

e.e. cummings, POET (1894-1962)

Family Appointments	Meals / Kitchen	Home
2 Saturday		
3 Sunday		

Messages

July

Family Appointments	Meals / Kitchen	Home	To Do
4 Monday *Independence Day (U.S.)*			
5 Tuesday			
6 Wednesday			
7 Thursday			
8 Friday			

JULY 2022

S	M	T	W	T	F	S
					1	2
3	**4**	**5**	**6**	**7**	**8**	**9**
10	11	12	13	14	15	16
17	18	19	20	21	22	23
24/31	25	26	27	28	29	30

There is no room for doubters when it comes to wishing. If you have difficulty believing in wishes with all your heart, take a close look at yourself in the mirror — you've probably turned into a grownup without realizing it.

David Greer, LAWYER & WISH SPECIALIST (1946-)

Family Appointments	Meals / Kitchen	Home
9 Saturday		
10 Sunday		

Messages

July

Family Appointments	Meals / Kitchen	Home	To Do
11 Monday			
12 Tuesday			
13 Wednesday ○ *Full Moon*			
14 Thursday			
15 Friday			

JULY 2022						
S	M	T	W	T	F	S
					1	2
3	**4**	5	6	7	8	9
10	**11**	**12**	**13**	**14**	**15**	**16**
17	18	19	20	21	22	23
24/31	25	26	27	28	29	30

In childhood, time is kind. A moment is swallowed whole, by senses open and able.

Nicoletta Baumeister, ARTIST (20TH C.)

Family Appointments	Meals / Kitchen	Home
16 Saturday		
17 Sunday		

Messages

July

Family Appointments	Meals / Kitchen	Home	To Do
18 Monday			
19 Tuesday			
20 Wednesday			
21 Thursday			
22 Friday			

POLESTAR FAMILY CALENDAR ™

JULY 2022

S	M	T	W	T	F	S
					1	2
3	**4**	5	6	7	8	9
10	11	12	13	14	15	16
17	**18**	**19**	**20**	**21**	**22**	**23**
24₃₁	25	26	27	28	29	30

Your mind will make you as crazy as you let it. Learn to recognize when you have slipped into "catastrophic thinking" mode and fight back.

Fawn Germer, INVESTIGATIVE JOURNALIST (20TH C.)

Family Appointments	Meals / Kitchen	Home

23 Saturday

24 Sunday

Messages

July

Family Appointments	Meals / Kitchen	Home	To Do
25 Monday			
26 Tuesday			
27 Wednesday			
28 Thursday ● *New Moon*			
29 Friday			

JULY 2022						
S	M	T	W	T	F	S
					1	2
3	**4**	5	6	7	8	9
10	11	12	13	14	15	16
17	18	19	20	21	22	23
24/31	**25**	**26**	**27**	**28**	**29**	**30**

AUGUST 2022						
S	M	T	W	T	F	S
	1	2	3	4	5	6
7	8	9	10	11	12	13
14	15	16	17	18	19	20
21	22	23	24	25	26	27
28	29	30	31			

Yellow butterflies look like flowers flying through the warm summer air.

Andrea Willis, (20TH C.)

Family Appointments	Meals / Kitchen	Home
30 Saturday		
31 Sunday		

Messages

August 2022

SUNDAY	MONDAY	TUESDAY	WEDNESDAY	THURSDAY	FRIDAY	SATURDAY
	Civic Holiday (Canada) 1	2	3	4	5	
7	8	9	10	*Full Moon* ○ 11	12	1
14	15	16	17	18	19	2
21	22	23	24	25	26	*New Moon* ● 2
28	29	30	31			

JULY

S	M	T	W	T	F	S
					1	2
3	4	5	6	7	8	9
10	11	12	13	14	15	16
17	18	19	20	21	22	23
24	25	26	27	28	29	30
31						

SEPTEMBER

S	M	T	W	T	F	S
				1	2	3
4	5	6	7	8	9	10
11	12	13	14	15	16	17
18	19	20	21	22	23	24
25	26	27	28	29	30	

ugust 2022

DO THIS MONTH

W PROJECTS/IDEAS

NOTES

August

Family Appointments	Meals / Kitchen	Home	To Do
1 Monday *Civic Holiday (Canada)*			
2 Tuesday			
3 Wednesday			
4 Thursday			
5 Friday			

POLESTAR FAMILY CALENDAR ™

AUGUST 2022

S	M	T	W	T	F	S
	1	**2**	**3**	**4**	**5**	**6**
7	8	9	10	11	12	13
14	15	16	17	18	19	20
21	22	23	24	25	26	27
28	29	30	31			

Sit still. Look around. Inhale life.
Come sit by the river.

Robert Genn, ARTIST (1936-2014)

Family Appointments	Meals / Kitchen	Home
6 Saturday		
7 Sunday		

Messages

August

Family Appointments	Meals / Kitchen	Home	To Do
8 Monday			
9 Tuesday			
10 Wednesday			
11 Thursday ○ *Full Moon*			
12 Friday			

AUGUST 2022

S	M	T	W	T	F	S
	1	2	3	4	5	6
7	**8**	**9**	**10**	**11**	**12**	**13**
14	15	16	17	18	19	20
21	22	23	24	25	26	27
28	29	30	31			

When we just take the time to stop and look upwards, the immensity of the night sky actually sinks in.

Bob McDonald, WRITER & JOURNALIST (1951-)

Family Appointments	Meals / Kitchen	Home

13 Saturday

14 Sunday

Messages

August

Family Appointments	Meals / Kitchen	Home	To Do
15 Monday			
16 Tuesday			
17 Wednesday			
18 Thursday			
19 Friday			

AUGUST 2022

S	M	T	W	T	F	S
	1	2	3	4	5	6
7	8	9	10	11	12	13
14	**15**	**16**	**17**	**18**	**19**	**20**
21	22	23	24	25	26	27
28	29	30	31			

When you try to repress a yawn,
it comes out of your ears.

Saul Steinberg, CARTOONIST (1914-1999)

Family Appointments	Meals / Kitchen	Home
20 Saturday		
21 Sunday		

Messages

August

Family Appointments	Meals / Kitchen	Home	To Do
22 Monday			
23 Tuesday			
24 Wednesday			
25 Thursday			
26 Friday			

AUGUST 2022

S	M	T	W	T	F	S
	1	2	3	4	5	6
7	8	9	10	11	12	13
14	15	16	17	18	19	20
21	**22**	**23**	**24**	**25**	**26**	**27**
28	29	30	31			

Poetry calls us to pause. There is so much we overlook, while the abundance around us continues to shimmer, on its own.

Naomi Shihab Nye, WRITER & POET (1952-)

Family Appointments	Meals / Kitchen	Home
27 Saturday ● *New Moon*		
28 Sunday		

Messages

September 2022

SUNDAY	MONDAY	TUESDAY	WEDNESDAY	THURSDAY	FRIDAY	SATURDAY
AUGUST S M T W T F S 　1 2 3 4 5 6 7 8 9 10 11 12 13 14 15 16 17 18 19 20 21 22 23 24 25 26 27 28 29 30 31	**OCTOBER** S M T W T F S 　　　　　　1 2 3 4 5 6 7 8 9 **10** 11 12 13 14 15 16 17 18 19 20 21 22 23 24 25 26 27 28 29 30 31			1	2	
4	*Labour Day* 5	6	7	8	9	*Full Moon* ○ 1
11	12	13	14	15	16	1
18	19	20	*U.N. International Day of Peace* 21	*Autumnal Equinox* 22	23	2
New Moon ● 25	*First day of Rosh Hashanah* 26	27	28	29	30	

eptember 2022

O DO THIS MONTH

EW PROJECTS/IDEAS

NOTES

August/September

Family Appointments	Meals / Kitchen	Home	To Do
29 Monday			
30 Tuesday			
31 Wednesday			
1 Thursday			
2 Friday			

AUGUST 2022

S	M	T	W	T	F	S
	1	2	3	4	5	6
7	8	9	10	11	12	13
14	15	16	17	18	19	20
21	22	23	24	25	26	27
28	**29**	**30**	**31**			

SEPTEMBER 2022

S	M	T	W	T	F	S
				1	**2**	**3**
4	**5**	6	7	8	9	10
11	12	13	14	15	16	17
18	19	20	21	22	23	24
25	26	27	28	29	30	

Procrastination is like a credit card; it's a lot of fun until you get the bill.

Christopher Parker, ACTOR (1983-)

Family Appointments	Meals / Kitchen	Home
3 Saturday		
4 Sunday		

Messages

September

Family Appointments	Meals / Kitchen	Home	To Do
5 Monday *Labour Day*			
6 Tuesday			
7 Wednesday			
8 Thursday			
9 Friday			

To Buy

SEPTEMBER 2022						
S	M	T	W	T	F	S
				1	2	3
4	**5**	**6**	**7**	**8**	**9**	**10**
11	12	13	14	15	16	17
18	19	20	21	22	23	24
25	26	27	28	29	30	

It has always seemed strange to me that in our endless discussions about education so little stress is laid on the pleasure of becoming an educated person, the enormous interest it adds to life.

Edith Hamilton, EDUCATOR (1867-1963)

Family Appointments	Meals / Kitchen	Home

10 Saturday ○ *Full Moon*

11 Sunday

Messages

September

Family Appointments	Meals / Kitchen	Home	To Do
12 Monday			
13 Tuesday			
14 Wednesday			
15 Thursday			
16 Friday			

CANADIAN ORDER FORM

The 2023 Polestar Family Calendar™ is now available. To find a local outlet please visit our website or call us at 1-800-296-6955. You can order by mail by sending in this form to the address below; by phone or order online. For more information on our other publications please visit our website at **www.polestarcalendars.com.**

* If you order 3 or more calendars deduct $1.95 per copy.

In BC, the total cost (*including postage and taxes*)
for one Family calendar is $25.36
In ON, one Family calendar is $25.93
In NS, NB, NL, PE one Family calendar is $26.39
Anywhere else in Canada, one Family calendar is $24.10

Please Note: Some stores do sell the calendar for less than the regular $17.95 retail price. We don't want to underprice the many other stores that sell our products and so sell it to you at the full retail price.

Visa/MasterCard payments:

Acct. # ____ ____ ____ ____

Exp. ___ / ___   CVV# ___ ___ ___

Name _____

Please make your cheque/money order payable in Canadian funds to:

Polestar Calendars Ltd.,
6518 Slocan River Rd.,
Winlaw, B.C. V0G 2J0
Phone 1-800-296-6955

# of Copies		Total
	(*For orders of 3 or more copies deduct $1.95/calendar**)	
____	2023 Polestar Family Calendar, $17.95	____
____	2023 Polestar Business Agenda, $19.95	____
____	2023 Polestar Planner, $14.95	____
____	Original Student Calendar (Aug. 2022), $13.95	____
Postage & Handling	Canada: $5.00 per copy	____
	International: $18.00 per copy	____
	Subtotal	____

Tax payable on Subtotal, please select the sales tax that applies: Tax payable

GST: 5% (AB, SK, MB, QC, YT, NT, NU)
GST: 5%/PST 7% (BC residents only – GST/PST due on calendar, GST due on postage)
HST: 13% (ON)
HST: 15% (NS, NB, NL, PE)   **Total Enclosed** ____

Send calendars to: *(please print)*

Name _____
Address _____
City/Town _____ Province _____ Postal Code _____
Email: _____ Phone _____

AMERICAN ORDER FORM

The 2023 Polestar Family Calendar™ is now available. To place your order please mail in this form to the address below, phone 1-800-296-6955, or order online.

For more information on our other publications please visit our website at **www.polestarcalendars.com.**

* If you order 3 or more calendars deduct $1.95 per copy.
i.e. 1 Business ($18), 1 Planner ($13), 1 Student ($11),
1 Family ($16) or 3 Family ($48)

Number of Copies		Total
	(For orders of 3 or more copies deduct $1.95/calenda*)	
_____	2023 Polestar Family Calendar, $17.95	_____
_____	2023 Polestar Business Agenda, $19.95	_____
_____	2023 Polestar Planner, $14.95	_____
_____	Original Student Calendar (Aug.2022), $13.95	_____
Postage & Handling	U.S.: $7.50 per copy	_____
	International: $17.00 per copy	_____
	Total Enclosed	_____

Visa/MasterCard payments:

Acct. # _ _ _ _ _ _ _ _ _ _ _ _ _ _ _ _

Exp. ____ / ____   CVV# ____

Name _____

Please make your check/money order
payable in U.S. funds to:

Polestar Calendars Ltd.,
6518 Slocan River Rd.,
Winlaw, B.C. Canada V0G 2J0
Phone 1-800-296-6955

Send calendars to: *(please print)*

Name _____

Address _____

City _____ State/Country _____ ZipCode _____

Email: _____ Phone _____

SEPTEMBER 2022

S	M	T	W	T	F	S
				1	2	3
4	**5**	6	7	8	9	10
11	**12**	**13**	**14**	**15**	**16**	**17**
18	19	20	21	22	23	24
25	26	27	28	29	30	

You cannot get through a single day without having an impact on the world around you.

Jane Goodall, PRIMATOLOGIST (1934-)

Family Appointments	Meals / Kitchen	Home
17 Saturday		
18 Sunday		

Messages

September

Family Appointments	Meals / Kitchen	Home		To Do
19 Monday				
20 Tuesday				
21 Wednesday *U.N. International Day of Peace*				
22 Thursday *Autumnal Equinox*				
23 Friday				

SEPTEMBER 2022

S	M	T	W	T	F	S
				1	2	3
4	**5**	6	7	8	9	10
11	12	13	14	15	16	17
18	**19**	**20**	**21**	**22**	**23**	**24**
25	26	27	28	29	30	

It's the first day of autumn! A time of hot chocolatey mornings, and toasty marshmallow evenings, and best of all, leaping into leaves!

Winnie-the-Pooh by A.A. Milne,
WRITER (1882-1956)

Family Appointments	Meals / Kitchen	Home
24 Saturday		
25 Sunday ● *New Moon*		

Messages

October 2022

SUNDAY	MONDAY	TUESDAY	WEDNESDAY	THURSDAY	FRIDAY	SATURDAY

SEPTEMBER

S	M	T	W	T	F	S
					1	2	3
4	5	6	7	8	9	10
11	12	13	14	15	16	17
18	19	20	21	22	23	24
25	26	27	28	29	30	

NOVEMBER

S	M	T	W	T	F	S
		1	2	3	4	5
6	7	8	9	10	11	12
13	14	15	16	17	18	19
20	21	22	23	24	25	26
27	28	29	30			

SUNDAY	MONDAY	TUESDAY	WEDNESDAY	THURSDAY	FRIDAY	SATURDAY
2	3	4	*Yom Kippur* 5	6	7	1
Full Moon ○ 9	*Thanksgiving Day (Canada), Columbus Day (U.S.)* 10	11	12	13	14	1
16	17	18	19	20	21	2
23	*Diwali* 24	*New Moon* ● 25	26	27	28	2
30	*Halloween* 31					

October 2022

NEW PROJECTS/IDEAS

NOTES

September/October

Family Appointments	Meals / Kitchen	Home	To Do
26 Monday *First day of Rosh Hashanah*			
27 Tuesday			
28 Wednesday			
29 Thursday			
30 Friday			

To Buy

SEPTEMBER 2022
S	M	T	W	T	F	S
				1	2	3
4	**5**	6	7	8	9	10
11	12	13	14	15	16	17
18	19	20	21	22	23	24
25	**26**	**27**	**28**	**29**	**30**	

OCTOBER 2022
S	M	T	W	T	F	S
						1
2	3	4	5	6	7	8
9	**10**	11	12	13	14	15
16	17	18	19	20	21	22
23/30	24/31	25	26	27	28	29

Silence is the source of
so much of what we need
to get through our lives.

Marilyn Nelson, POET (1946-)

Family Appointments	Meals / Kitchen	Home
1 Saturday		
2 Sunday		

Messages

October

Family Appointments	Meals / Kitchen	Home	To Do
3 Monday			
4 Tuesday			
5 Wednesday *Yom Kippur*			
6 Thursday			
7 Friday			

OCTOBER 2022

S	M	T	W	T	F	S
						1
2	**3**	**4**	**5**	**6**	**7**	**8**
9	**10**	11	12	13	14	15
16	17	18	19	20	21	22
23 30	24 31	25	26	27	28	29

What we would like to do is change the world —
make it a little simpler for people to feed, clothe,
and shelter themselves.

Dorothy Day, JOURNALIST & ACTIVIST (1897-1980)

Family Appointments	Meals / Kitchen	Home
8 Saturday		
9 Sunday ○ *Full Moon*		

Messages

October

Family Appointments	Meals / Kitchen	Home	To Do
10 Monday *Thanksgiving Day (Canada), Columbus Day (U.S.)*			
11 Tuesday			
12 Wednesday			
13 Thursday			
14 Friday			

OCTOBER 2022

S	M	T	W	T	F	S
						1
2	3	4	5	6	7	8
9	**10**	**11**	**12**	**13**	**14**	**15**
16	17	18	19	20	21	22
23 30	24 31	25	26	27	28	29

Autumn burned brightly, a running flame through the mountains, a torch flung to the trees.

Faith Baldwin, WRITER (1893-1978)

Family Appointments	Meals / Kitchen	Home

15 Saturday

16 Sunday

Messages

October

Family Appointments	Meals / Kitchen	Home	To Do
17 Monday			
18 Tuesday			
19 Wednesday			
20 Thursday			
21 Friday			

POLESTAR FAMILY CALENDAR ™

OCTOBER 2022

S	M	T	W	T	F	S
						1
2	3	4	5	6	7	8
9	**10**	11	12	13	14	15
16	**17**	**18**	**19**	**20**	**21**	**22**
23₃₀	²⁴₃₁	25	26	27	28	29

Stop thinking or acting like life will happen
after everything is crossed off your list.

Nancy McFadden, POLITICAL ADVISOR (1958-2018)

Family Appointments	Meals / Kitchen	Home
22 Saturday		
23 Sunday		

Messages

October

Family Appointments	Meals / Kitchen	Home
24 Monday *Diwali*		
25 Tuesday ● *New Moon*		
26 Wednesday		
27 Thursday		
28 Friday		

To Do

OCTOBER 2022

S	M	T	W	T	F	S
						1
2	3	4	5	6	7	8
9	**10**	11	12	13	14	15
16	17	18	19	20	21	22
23 30	24 31	**25**	**26**	**27**	**28**	**29**

Today's plan: snuggling with the dogs.
Sundays are all about setting achievable goals.

Angie Abdou, WRITER (1969-)

Family Appointments	Meals / Kitchen	Home
29 Saturday		
30 Sunday		

Messages

November 2022

SUNDAY	MONDAY	TUESDAY	WEDNESDAY	THURSDAY	FRIDAY	SATURDAY
		1	2	3	4	
Daylight Saving Time ends 6	7	*Full Moon* ○ 8	9	10	*Remembrance Day (Canada), Veterans' Day (U.S.)* 11	1
13	14	15	16	17	18	1
Universal Children's Day 20	21	22	*New Moon* ● 23	*Thanksgiving Day (U.S.)* 24	25	2
27	28	29	30			

OCTOBER

S	M	T	W	T	F	S
						1
2	3	4	5	6	7	8
9	**10**	11	12	13	14	15
16	17	18	19	20	21	22
23	24	25	26	27	28	29
30	31					

DECEMBER

S	M	T	W	T	F	
				1	2	
4	5	6	7	8	9	1
11	12	13	14	15	16	1
18	19	20	21	22	23	2
25	**26**	27	28	29	30	3

November 2022

W PROJECTS/IDEAS

NOTES

October/November

Family Appointments	Meals / Kitchen	Home	To Do
31 Monday *Halloween*			
1 Tuesday			
2 Wednesday			
3 Thursday			
4 Friday			

OCTOBER 2022

S	M	T	W	T	F	S
						1
2	3	4	5	6	7	8
9	**10**	11	12	13	14	15
16	17	18	19	20	21	22
23 30	24 31	25	26	27	28	29

NOVEMBER 2022

S	M	T	W	T	F	S
	1	**2**	**3**	**4**	**5**	
6	7	8	9	10	**11**	12
13	14	15	16	17	18	19
20	21	22	23	**24**	25	26
27	28	29	30			

Never put off until tomorrow
the fun you can have today.

Aldous Huxley,
WRITER (1894-1963)

Family Appointments	Meals / Kitchen	Home

5 Saturday

6 Sunday   *Daylight Saving Time ends*

Messages

November

	Family Appointments	Meals / Kitchen	Home	To Do
7 Monday				
8 Tuesday ○ *Full Moon*				
9 Wednesday				
10 Thursday				
11 Friday *Remembrance Day (Canada), Veterans' Day (U.S.)*				

NOVEMBER 2022

S	M	T	W	T	F	S
		1	2	3	4	5
6	**7**	**8**	**9**	**10**	**11**	**12**
13	14	15	16	17	18	19
20	21	22	23	**24**	25	26
27	28	29	30			

I dance anywhere. I just start moving my feet.

Savion Glover, DANCER (1973-)

Family Appointments	Meals / Kitchen	Home
12 Saturday		
13 Sunday		

Messages

November

Family Appointments	Meals / Kitchen	Home	To Do
14 Monday			
15 Tuesday			
16 Wednesday			
17 Thursday			
18 Friday			

NOVEMBER 2022

S	M	T	W	T	F	S
		1	2	3	4	5
6	7	8	9	10	**11**	12
13	**14**	**15**	**16**	**17**	**18**	**19**
20	21	22	23	**24**	25	26
27	28	29	30			

If I am an advocate for anything, it is to move.
As far as you can, as much as you can.
Across the ocean, or simply across the river.

Anthony Bourdain, CHEF & WRITER (1956-2018)

Family Appointments	Meals / Kitchen	Home
19 Saturday		
20 Sunday *Universal Children's Day*		

Messages

November

Family Appointments	Meals / Kitchen	Home	To Do
21 Monday			
22 Tuesday			
23 Wednesday ● *New Moon*			
24 Thursday *Thanksgiving Day (U.S.)*			
25 Friday			

To Buy

NOVEMBER 2022

S	M	T	W	T	F	S
		1	2	3	4	5
6	7	8	9	10	**11**	12
13	14	15	16	17	18	19
20	**21**	**22**	**23**	**24**	**25**	**26**
27	28	29	30			

Forget sale price. Everything is 100% off
when you don't buy it.

Joshua Fields Millburn, WRITER (1981-)

Family Appointments	Meals / Kitchen	Home
26 Saturday		
27 Sunday		

Messages

December 2022

SUNDAY	MONDAY	TUESDAY	WEDNESDAY	THURSDAY	FRIDAY	SATURDAY
NOVEMBER S M T W T F S 　　1 2 3 4 5 6 7 8 9 10 **11** 12 13 14 15 16 17 18 19 20 21 22 23 **24** 25 26 27 28 29 30	**JANUARY** S M T W T F S **1** 2 3 4 5 6 7 8 9 10 11 12 13 14 15 16 17 18 19 20 21 22 23 24 25 26 27 28 29 30 31			1	2	
4	5	6	*Full Moon* ○ 7	8	9	1(
11	12	13	14	15	16	1'
18	*First day of Hanukkah* 19	20	*Winter Solstice* 21	22	*New Moon* ● 23	2.
Christmas Day 25	*Boxing Day (Canada)* 26	27	28	29	30	*New Year's Eve* 3

ecember 2022

DO THIS MONTH

W PROJECTS/IDEAS

NOTES

November/December

Family Appointments	Meals / Kitchen	Home	To Do
28 Monday			
29 Tuesday			
30 Wednesday			
1 Thursday			
2 Friday			

NOVEMBER 2022

S	M	T	W	T	F	S
		1	2	3	4	5
6	7	8	9	10	**11**	12
13	14	15	16	17	18	19
20	21	22	23	**24**	25	26
27	**28**	**29**	**30**			

DECEMBER 2022

S	M	T	W	T	F	S
				1	**2**	**3**
4	5	6	7	8	9	10
11	12	13	14	15	16	17
18	19	20	21	22	23	24
25	**26**	27	28	29	30	31

Listen with an open heart
and an empathetic ear.

Micah Eames,
WRITER & ACTIVIST (20TH C.)

Family Appointments	Meals / Kitchen	Home
3 Saturday		
4 Sunday		

Messages

December

Family Appointments	Meals / Kitchen	Home	To Do
5 Monday			
6 Tuesday			
7 Wednesday ○ *Full Moon*			
8 Thursday			
9 Friday			

DECEMBER 2022

S	M	T	W	T	F	S
				1	2	3
4	**5**	**6**	**7**	**8**	**9**	**10**
11	12	13	14	15	16	17
18	19	20	21	22	23	24
25	**26**	27	28	29	30	31

I think that the more we take care of the person next to us and across the street, the better off we're going to be.

Rachelle Leblanc, DESIGNER (1985-)

Family Appointments	Meals / Kitchen	Home
10 Saturday		
11 Sunday		

Messages

December

Family Appointments	Meals / Kitchen	Home	To Do
12 Monday			
13 Tuesday			
14 Wednesday			
15 Thursday			
16 Friday			

DECEMBER 2022

S	M	T	W	T	F	S
				1	2	3
4	5	6	7	8	9	10
11	**12**	**13**	**14**	**15**	**16**	**17**
18	19	20	21	22	23	24
25	**26**	27	28	29	30	31

Just because things hadn't gone the way I had planned
didn't necessarily mean they had gone wrong.

Ann Patchett, WRITER (1963-)

Family Appointments	Meals / Kitchen	Home
17 Saturday		
18 Sunday		

Messages

December

Family Appointments	Meals / Kitchen	Home	To Do
19 Monday *First day of Hanukkah*			
20 Tuesday			
21 Wednesday *Winter Solstice*			
22 Thursday			
23 Friday ● *New Moon*			

DECEMBER 2022

S	M	T	W	T	F	S
				1	2	3
4	5	6	7	8	9	10
11	12	13	14	15	16	17
18	**19**	**20**	**21**	**22**	**23**	**24**
25	**26**	27	28	29	30	31

Snow was falling,
so much like stars
filling the dark trees
that one could easily imagine
its reason for being was nothing more
than prettiness.

Mary Oliver, POET (1935-2019)

Family Appointments	Meals / Kitchen	Home
24 Saturday		
25 Sunday *Christmas Day*		

Messages

December/January

Family Appointments	Meals / Kitchen	Home
26 Monday *Boxing Day (Canada)*		
27 Tuesday		
28 Wednesday		
29 Thursday		
30 Friday		

To Do

To Buy

DECEMBER 2022

S	M	T	W	T	F	S
				1	2	3
4	5	6	7	8	9	10
11	12	13	14	15	16	17
18	19	20	21	22	23	24
25	**26**	**27**	**28**	**29**	**30**	**31**

JANUARY 2023

S	M	T	W	T	F	S
1	2	3	4	5	6	7
8	9	10	11	12	13	14
15	16	17	18	19	20	21
22	23	24	25	26	27	28
29	30	31				

There is kindness yet in this world, and hope for us all.

Claudia Rankine, POET (1963-)

Family Appointments	Meals / Kitchen	Home
31 Saturday *New Year's Eve*		
1 Sunday *New Year's Day*		

Messages

January

Family Appointments	Meals / Kitchen	Home	To Do
2 Monday			
3 Tuesday			
4 Wednesday			
5 Thursday			
6 Friday ○ *Full Moon*			

JANUARY 2023

S	M	T	W	T	F	S
1	**2**	**3**	**4**	**5**	**6**	**7**
8	9	10	11	12	13	14
15	16	17	18	19	20	21
22	23	24	25	26	27	28
29	30	31				

To look back all the time is boring.
Excitement lies in tomorrow!

Natalia Makrova, DANCER (1940-)

Family Appointments	Meals / Kitchen	Home
7 Saturday		
8 Sunday		

Messages

January 2023

SUNDAY	MONDAY	TUESDAY	WEDNESDAY	THURSDAY	FRIDAY	SATURDAY
New Year's Day 1	2	3	4	5	*Full Moon* ○ 6	
8	9	10	11	12	13	1.
15	*Martin Luther* 16 *King, Jr. Day (U.S.)*	17	18	19	20	*New Moon* ● 2
22	23	24	25	26	27	2
29	30	31				

DECEMBER

S	M	T	W	T	F	S
				1	2	3
4	5	6	7	8	9	10
11	12	13	14	15	16	17
18	19	20	21	22	23	24
25	**26**	27	28	29	30	31

FEBRUARY

S	M	T	W	T	F	
			1	2	3	
5	6	7	8	9	10	1
12	13	14	15	16	17	1
19	**20**	21	22	23	24	2
26	27	28				

DO THIS MONTH

V PROJECTS/IDEAS

NOTES

2023 Planning Calendar

JANUARY

S	M	T	W	T	F	S
1	2	3	4	5	6	7
8	9	10	11	12	13	14
15	16	17	18	19	20	21
22	23	24	25	26	27	28
29	30	31				

FEBRUARY

S	M	T	W	T	F	S
			1	2	3	4
5	6	7	8	9	10	11
12	13	14	15	16	17	18
19	**20**	21	22	23	24	25
26	27	28				

MARCH

S	M	T	W	T	F	S
			1	2	3	
5	6	7	8	9	10	1
12	13	14	15	16	17	1
19	20	21	22	23	24	2
26	27	28	29	30	31	

APRIL

S	M	T	W	T	F	S
						1
2	3	4	5	6	**7**	8
9	10	11	12	13	14	15
16	17	18	19	20	21	22
23	24	25	26	27	28	29
30						

MAY

S	M	T	W	T	F	S
	1	2	3	4	5	6
7	8	9	10	11	12	13
14	15	16	17	18	19	20
21	**22**	23	24	25	26	27
28	**29**	30	31			

JUNE

S	M	T	W	T	F	S
				1	2	
4	5	6	7	8	9	1
11	12	13	14	15	16	1
18	19	20	21	22	23	2
25	26	27	28	29	30	

23 Planning Calendar

JULY

S	M	T	W	T	F	S
						1
2	3	**4**	5	6	7	8
9	10	11	12	13	14	15
5	17	18	19	20	21	22
3	24	25	26	27	28	29
0	31					

AUGUST

S	M	T	W	T	F	S
		1	2	3	4	5
6	**7**	8	9	10	11	12
13	14	15	16	17	18	19
20	21	22	23	24	25	26
27	28	29	30	31		

SEPTEMBER

S	M	T	W	T	F	S
					1	2
3	**4**	5	6	7	8	9
10	11	12	13	14	15	16
17	18	19	20	21	22	23
24	25	26	27	28	29	30

OCTOBER

S	M	T	W	T	F	S
1	2	3	4	5	6	7
3	**9**	10	11	12	13	14
5	16	17	18	19	20	21
2	23	24	25	26	27	28
9	30	31				

NOVEMBER

S	M	T	W	T	F	S
			1	2	3	4
5	6	7	8	9	10	**11**
12	13	14	15	16	17	18
19	20	21	22	**23**	24	25
26	27	28	29	30		

DECEMBER

S	M	T	W	T	F	S
					1	2
3	4	5	6	7	8	9
10	11	12	13	14	15	16
17	18	19	20	21	22	23
24	**25**	**26**	27	28	29	30
31						

Family Profiles

Name			Wish List
Birthday	Favourite Colours		
Other Special Days			
Measurements & Clothing Sizes	Favourite Foods	Other Favourites	

Name			Wish List
Birthday	Favourite Colours		
Other Special Days			
Measurements & Clothing Sizes	Favourite Foods	Other Favourites	

Name			Wish List
Birthday	Favourite Colours		
Other Special Days			
Measurements & Clothing Sizes	Favourite Foods	Other Favourites	

mily Profiles

me				Wish List
thday	Favourite Colours			
her Special Days				
surements & Clothing Sizes	Favourite Foods	Other Favourites		

me				Wish List
rthday	Favourite Colours			
her Special Days				
surements & Clothing Sizes	Favourite Foods	Other Favourites		

me				Wish List
rthday	Favourite Colours			
her Special Days				
surements & Clothing Sizes	Favourite Foods	Other Favourites		

Family Profiles

Name			Wish List
Birthday	Favourite Colours		
Other Special Days			
Measurements & Clothing Sizes	Favourite Foods	Other Favourites	

Name			Wish List
Birthday	Favourite Colours		
Other Special Days			
Measurements & Clothing Sizes	Favourite Foods	Other Favourites	

Name			Wish List
Birthday	Favourite Colours		
Other Special Days			
Measurements & Clothing Sizes	Favourite Foods	Other Favourites	

tes To Remember

Date	Event/Occasion

Date	Event/Occasion

Items Loaned

Date	Item	Loaned To	Return Dat

Make a note in the calendar when the item should be returned.
When the item is returned, cross it off this list.

ms Borrowed

Date	Item	Borrowed From	Return Date

Make a note in the calendar when the item should be returned.
When the item is returned, cross it off this list.

Storage Record

Date	Item	Where Stored

List storage location of seasonal or seldom used items: sports equipment, tools, clothing, holiday and party supplies. Also note location of important documents such as medical records, insurance policies, wills, appliance warranties.

otes

Notes

Notes

Notes

otes

Notes

Phone List

Name	Phone/Email	Address

Phone List

Name	Phone/Email	Address

hone List

Name	Phone/Email	Address

Phone List

Name	Phone/Email	Address

To Buy

Polestar Family Calendar

To Buy

Polestar Family Calendar

To Buy

Polestar Family Calendar

To Buy

Polestar Family Calendar

To Buy

Polestar Family Calendar

To Buy

Polestar Family Calendar

To Buy

Polestar Family Calendar

To Buy

Polestar Family Calendar

To Buy

Polestar Family Calendar

To Buy

Polestar Family Calendar

To Buy

Polestar Family Calendar

To Buy

Polestar Family Calendar

To Buy

Polestar Family Calendar

To Buy

Polestar Family Calendar

To Buy

Polestar Family Calendar

To Buy

Polestar Family Calendar

To Buy

Polestar Family Calendar

To Buy

Polestar Family Calendar

To Buy

Polestar Family Calendar

To Buy

Polestar Family Calendar

To Buy

Polestar Family Calendar

To Buy

Polestar Family Calendar

To Buy

Polestar Family Calendar

To Buy

Polestar Family Calendar

To Buy

To Buy

To Buy

Polestar Family Calendar

Polestar Family Calendar

Polestar Family Calendar

To Buy

To Buy

To Buy

Polestar Family Calendar

Polestar Family Calendar

Polestar Family Calendar